Consultant Iain Bain, Editor, the
Geographical Magazine
Managing Editor Belinda Hollyer
Editor Beverley Birch
Design Jerry Watkiss
Picture Research Kathy Lockley
Production Rosemary Bishop
Illustrations John Shackell
          Ron Hayward
          John Mousdale
          Marilyn Day
          Tony Payne
          Raymond Turvey
Maps Matthews & Taylor Associates
(pages 44–45)

Photographic sources Key to positions of
illustrations: (T) top, (C) center, (B) bottom,
(L) left, (R) right.
Aldus Archive 22(T), 29(B); Dennis Moore
10(T), 11(T), 20(T), 31(TR), 33(TR),
34(T). All-Sport Cover. Laura Ashley 28(T).
Australian Information Service 40(BL). Nick
Birch 8(BL), 11(B), 30–1(T), 31(BL),
32–3(T), 35(T), 35(B), 36–7, 38(BL),
40–1(T). BBC Hulton 17(BR), 19(TL),
19(TR), 21(BL), 23(BR), 26(T), 27(TL).

British Hovercraft Corporation 27(BR).
British Museum 18(BR). British Tourist
Association Contents page, 25(BR),
28–9(B), 37(BR), 41(BL). Butlins 32(B).
Central Office of Information 15(BR).
Colchester Archaeological Trust 12(B).
Colorsport 40(BR). Daily Telegraph Colour
Library Cover. Robert Estall 24. Mary
Evans Picture Library 12–13, 14(BR), 16,
18(BL), 19(BL), 26(BL), 27(TR). Sally &
Richard Greenhill 22(B), 34(B), 34–5(B),
38–9(B). Sonia Halliday Endpapers, 8(T),
8(BR), 13(BR), 23(TL), 23(BL), 39(BR).
Robert Harding Picture Library 28(B),
29(T), 33(BL). Impact Photos 31(BR),
41(BR). David Muscroft Photography
41(TR). National Coal Board 20(C).
National Gallery 23(TR). National Portrait
Gallery 14(BL), 15(BL). Popperfoto 25(TR),
26–7(B). Power Pix 21(BR). Rex Features
10(B), 21(T). Ann Ronan Picture Library
16–17. Sefton Photo Library 17(TL).
Scotsman Publications 20(B), 38–9(T).
Scottish Tourist Board 33(BR).

14–15(T) Reproduced by gracious permission
of Her Majesty Queen Elizabeth II
Impreso por:
Edime, Org. Gráfica, S. A.
(Móstoles) MADRID

Encuaderna: Larmor, S. A.
(Móstoles) MADRID

Depósito Legal: M. 41536-1986
I.S.B.N.: 84-599-1848-3

IMPRESO EN ESPAÑA
PRINTED IN SPAIN

**Library of Congress
Cataloging-in-Publication Data**

Sproule, Anna.
  Great Britain, the land and its people.

  (Silver Burdett countries)
  Includes index.
  Summary: An introduction to the people
and way of life in England, Scotland, and
Wales—the countries making up Great Britain.
  1. Great Britain—Juvenile literature.
[1. Great Britain]
  I. Title. II. Series.
DA27.5.S67 1987 941 86-24868
ISBN 0-382-09254-6

Silver Burdett
Countries

Great Britain

the land and its people

Anna Sproule

Silver Burdett Press
Morristown, New Jersey

Contents

A land of rich variety

Mountains, lakes, and coastlines

Great Britain is made up of three countries—England, Scotland, and Wales. With Northern Ireland, it forms the United Kingdom.

It is a land of tremendous variety. Its landscapes range from mountains, lakes, and forests, especially in Wales and Scotland, to flat plains, some of them below sea level. It contains the rolling pastoral country of central England and the bleak moorlands of Devon and Cornwall in the southwest. Some coastlines are rocky; others are lined with miles of sandy beaches. On Britain's highest peak, Ben Nevis in northwestern Scotland, there may be snow for much of the year.

Visitors to Great Britain are often surprised by the wide variety in its countryside. They are also surprised by how small Britain is. But, with an average of 325 people living in each square mile, it is one of the most crowded countries in the world.

▲ The valley of Glencoe in the Scottish Highlands, the scene of the massacre of 38 people in 1692. It is an important center for tourism and activities like climbing, walking, and skiing.

▼ Visiting Britain by bicycle. In count areas many people must rely on their ow transportation to go about their daily live Three-quarters of Britain is still thinly-pop lated open country.

▲ The London borough of Croydon is less thickly populated than some of the inner areas of London. But, with its population of over 300,000, it still has more people per square mile than most other areas in Britain.

Everyone in Britain probably knows at least one area very well indeed: their own. But the 14 million or so visitors who come to Britain every year may well have the best idea of what the whole country really looks like. The map shows just some of the things that interest them, from Scotland right down to the southern coast of England.

SCOTLAND
1. St. Andrew's Cross, flag of Scotland.
2. Tartan of Macleod.
3. Tartan of Macgregor.
4. Loch Ness, home of the legendary monster, near Inverness.
5. "Bonnie Prince Charlie" (Charles Stuart). In 1745 he tried—unsuccessfully—to make himself king of Britain.
6. Ben Nevis, highest point in Britain (4,406 feet).
7. Scottish castle of the type found from the Borders northward.
8. Oil rig in the North Sea.

NORTH ENGLAND
9. Coin showing Britannia, issued by the Roman Emperor Hadrian.
10. Hadrian's Wall at Haltcastle.
11. The Venerable Bede, "father of English history," worked at Jarrow.
12. Holy Island (Lindisfarne), home of early Christian monks.
13. Longstone Lighthouse and Grace Darling, who heroically rescued sailors from a sinking ship in 1838.

EAST ANGLIA
14. The tulip fields of Lincolnshire.
15. Flat Fenland landscape.
16. Windmills in Suffolk and Norfolk.
17. Reed harvest in Norfolk.
18. Thatchwork on a Norfolk cottage.

THE MIDLANDS
19. Warwickshire, home of Shakespeare.
20. House of Tudor period, Stratford.
21. Warwickshire landscape.
22. Staffordshire, pottery center.
23. Oxford University.
24. Great Tom Tower, Oxford.

WALES
25. Harlech Castle.
26. National dress of Wales.
27. The mountains of Snowdonia.
28. The Welsh dragon, symbol of Wales.

SOUTHERN ENGLAND
29. Oast houses for drying hops, Kent.
30. Kent, "garden of England."
31. Banner of the Cinque Ports.
32. Dover Castle, Kent.
33. South coast piers.
34. White cliffs of Sussex and Kent.

WEST COUNTRY
35. Nineteenth-century tin mine.
36. Tourist beaches in Cornwall.
37. St. Michael's Mount, Cornwall.
38. The harbor of Polperro.

Languages and beliefs

Who are the people of Britain?

In 1981, when the last census count was held, there were 54 million Britons living in Great Britain. But very few of them would have called themselves that. The people of Britain tend to think of themselves not as British or Britons, but as English, Welsh, or Scottish.

Most of Britain's population comes from families that have lived somewhere in the country for many generations. Their main language is English—although some of them also speak the quite different Celtic languages of Welsh, Gaelic, Manx Gaelic, or Cornish. But some of the British come from families that have arrived in Britain since the Second World War. For example, their original family homes were in India, Pakistan, Bangladesh, in the West Indies, or different parts of the Mediterranean, and many still speak the languages used there. The different religions of those who have settled in Britain also recall their countries of family origin, and include Islam and Hinduism. A majority of the British are Christians.

Lincoln Cathedral, one of the finest reli-
us buildings in Great Britain. The traditional
gion of Britain is Christianity. When Lincoln
thedral was begun, in 1072, British Chris-
ns were all Roman Catholic. Now many
ong to the Protestant Churches, such as
Church of England and the Church of
otland.

During its history, Britain has exported
main language all over the world.

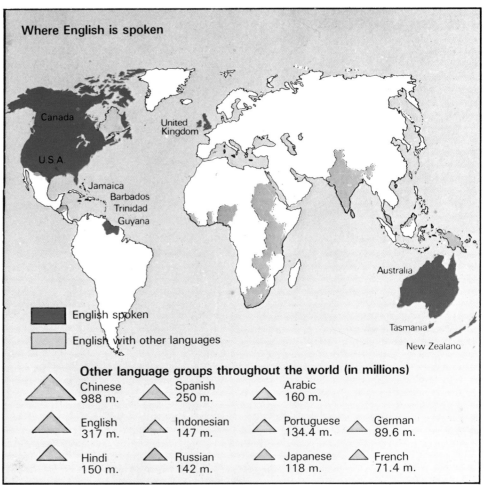

Where English is spoken

English spoken

English with other languages

Other language groups throughout the world (in millions)

Chinese 988 m.	Spanish 250 m.	Arabic 160 m.	
English 317 m.	Indonesian 147 m.	Portuguese 134.4 m.	German 89.6 m.
Hindi 150 m.	Russian 142 m.	Japanese 118 m.	French 71.4 m.

A Londoner of West Indian descent
dresses passersby in Hyde Park. Although
place of family origin is thousands of miles
ay, his language, like that of his listeners,
English.

From the early 1950s on, people from
ny countries in Asia, Africa, and the West
ies came to Britain to find work. They set-
d in British cities like London and Birming-
m. Many are Muslims, and worship at
sques like this one in London.

Queen Elizabeth II with the Dean of
ndsor. Queen Elizabeth is head of the
urch of England, the largest group of Prot-
ant worshipers in Britain. Other Protestant
urches include the Methodist Church and
Church of Scotland.

The makings of the British

Invasion and settlement

Until about 8000 BC, much of Britain had been covered by ice sheets and glaciers. The few thousand people who arrived there at the end of the last Ice Age were hunters and fishers who used stone and bone tools.

When the ice melted, the sea level rose and Britain became an island. Settlers who crossed from Europe brought new ways and equipment with them and, from about 3500 BC, the British began to become farmers.

Later settlers introduced another important change: the use of tools made of metal rather than stone. First bronze was used. Then, from around 550 BC, iron was introduced. During this whole period, Britain was being settled by a new group of skilled farmers and fighters who came from Central Europe. These people were called the Celts.

In 55 BC, the Roman leader Julius Caesar made a brief raid on Celtic Britain. But it was not until AD 43, under the Emperor Claudius, that the Romans finally conquered the British Celts. Only the Scottish Highlands remained outside Roman control.

The end of Roman Britain

The rule of the Romans lasted until AD 410, when the Roman troops left. Soon tribes from northern Europe—Angles, Saxons, and Jutes—began to invade the eastern part of Britain. The Romanized British fought back but, in the end, they were forced to move westward into remoter areas such as Wales. Later, in the 8th century, the Anglo-Saxons began to be invaded by the Viking raiders and traders of Scandinavia.

The last invasion came in 1066, when William of Normandy (William the Conqueror) defeated the Saxons and made himself king of England. But Wales did not give in to Norman rule until 1282. Scotland remained a separate kingdom.

▼ In the sunlight again after more than 1600 years: the skeletons of a man (right) and a woman (left) of Roman Britain are examined by an archaeologist in a Roman cemetery at Colchester.

The Romans invade Britain. There were
two Roman invasions: Julius Caesar's in 55 BC
(shown here), and the invasion of the Emperor
Claudius in AD 43.

Stonehenge was finally completed by
about 1750 BC. It is the earliest major work of
British architecture which has survived. The
architects were people who lived during
Britain's Bronze Age.

▲ A Saxon. After the Romans had aban-
doned Britain in the 5th century AD, Angles
and Jutes from Denmark and Saxons from
Germany conquered and gradually settled the
country. The Saxons started their raids while
the Romans were still in Britain; for defense,
Roman forts were built along the Saxon (or
east) coast.

▲ A Viking of the 8th century AD. The
Vikings are usually depicted as raiders who
later settled and became farmers. Recently,
however, experts have begun to think that
they came to Britain also as traders, and were
quite a sophisticated group of people.

▲ A Norman soldier of William the Conquer-
or's army. Soldiers like this, who fought the
troops of the Saxon King Harold, were re-
warded with gifts of land to live on.

The monarchs of Britain

Under one rule

Britain is a monarchy: the headship of state is an office into which the holder is born rather than elected, and which carries the ancient title of "king" or "queen." The British monarchy started in 1603. Originally there were separate rulers for England, Scotland, and Wales.

After the Romans left in AD 410, Britain became a collection of small independent kingdoms. The first to bring the English under his rule was Egbert, who died in 839. The monarchy he founded was continued by his successors, among them Alfred the Great. It was continued, too, by the last invader of Britain, William the Conqueror. His descendants continued to rule for almost a century, followed by a family, the Plantagenets, who were related by marriage. During the Plantagenets' long period in power, Wales was annexed.

Another important development came in 1603. King James VI of Scotland then became King James I of England on the death of Elizabeth I, last of the Tudor monarchs. He first used the title "King of Great Britain," although there was no union of the Scottish and the English parliaments until 1707.

The monarch's power challenged

First it was the noblemen who tried to challenge the power of the monarch. Later it was Parliament, which voiced the needs of the rich merchants. The biggest challenge came with the Civil War of 1642–8, which led to the execution of King Charles I and the abolition of the monarchy. (It was restored in 1660.) The last monarch to make a serious attempt to control Parliament was George III. Since his death in 1820, British monarchs have "reigned, but not ruled." The real power lies with Britain's government, led by the prime minister.

▲ Alfred the Great, king of Wessex in the south and west of England. He ruled at the time of the invasions by various groups from Scandinavia, and succeeded in keeping the invaders out of Wessex.

◄ The Virgin Queen, or "Good Queen Bess": Elizabeth I of England, greatest of the Tudor monarchs and one of the most able rulers Britain has ever had. During her reign (1558-1603) society became more stable, the arts flourished, and England became the foremost power in Europe.

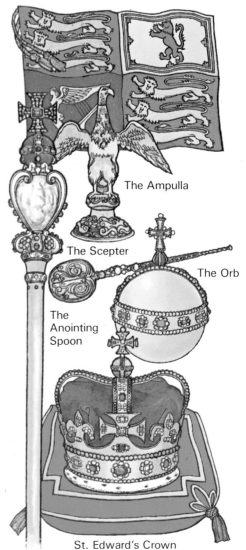

▼ The Royal Standard of Britain (the lion of England, the Welsh harp and the lion of Scotland), and the English coronation regalia, kept in the Tower of London.

The Ampulla

The Scepter

The Orb

The Anointing Spoon

St. Edward's Crown

▲ At home with the royal family in the 18th century: King George III with his wife, Queen Charlotte, and six of their children. George III aimed to recapture the power of the British monarch. For a while he succeeded in ruling through Parliament by bribing his supporters there to do what he wanted.

▼ The British monarch in the 20th century: Queen Elizabeth II, here seen on tour in the West Indies in 1966. As well as being the sovereign of the United Kingdom of Great Britain and Northern Ireland, she is also head of the Commonwealth.

▲ Mary Stuart, Queen of Scots, Elizabeth's cousin and a Catholic. Catholics saw her as Elizabeth's rival for the English throne. She was thus a source of danger to Elizabeth's Protestant government and Elizabeth had her executed. But, after Elizabeth's death, Mary's son, James VI of Scotland, also became England's ruler.

15

The British revolutions

More food for less work

After the Civil War of the 1640s, Great Britain never had another armed revolution similar to that of, for example, France or Russia. But its people led two revolutions of a different sort that changed the lives of almost everyone in the world.

The first one, which started in the late 17th century, was a revolution in agricultural methods. Over the next hundred years, British landowners and farmers made enormous strides in producing more food for less work. They did this by, for example, improving the quality of their breeds of livestock and developing new farm machinery and farming systems.

Steam, water, and factories

This Agricultural Revolution had two very important effects. Over the years, the growth in food supply meant a growth in population. But farming now

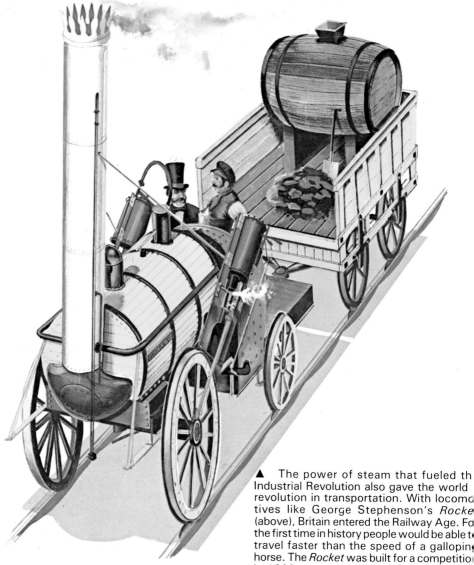

▲ The power of steam that fueled th Industrial Revolution also gave the world revolution in transportation. With locomo tives like George Stephenson's *Rocke* (above), Britain entered the Railway Age. Fo the first time in history people would be able t travel faster than the speed of a gallopin horse. The *Rocket* was built for a competitio in 1829.

▲ As the Industrial Revolution gathered pace, its machinery got larger and more powerful. The machine shown here is a hammer worked by steam, the invention of an engineer called James Nasmyth.

used less labor and fewer people were needed to produce the nation's food. They were therefore free for (and desperately needed) other work.

Improved farming implements were not the only British technological advances of the 1700s. Others were Newcomen's pumping engine run by steam, and Arkwright's spinning machine run on waterpower. The harnessing of these two kinds of power to machines led to the growth of "manufactories," in which goods could be made much more quickly than they ever could by hand. This was the second British revolution.

Although the factories of the Industrial Revolution put many old-style craftsmen out of jobs, they gave work to huge numbers of people to whom farming no longer offered a living. They also formed the base on which the wealth of Great Britain and the other industrialized countries of the world would grow.

The Industrial Revolution brought home wealth and power to Britain. But to many of the people who labored in its factories it also brought appalling working and living conditions; pollution of air, water, and land was another of its legacies.

▲ New farming methods made landowners more prosperous; the trim buildings of this village date from Coke's century.

▼ One of Britain's great agricultural reformers: Thomas Coke (pronounced "Cook"), Earl of Leicester. He owned a large estate in West Norfolk. When he took it over in 1776, it was poor farming land, but he increased its value enormously by improving farming methods.

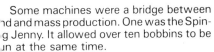

Some machines were a bridge between hand and mass production. One was the Spinning Jenny. It allowed over ten bobbins to be spun at the same time.

Queen-Empress: the age of Queen Victoria

Wealth and power

By the 19th century, the powers of the British monarch were more limited than they had been. But, all the same, Queen Victoria acted in the style of a great ruler. Her husband, German-born Prince Albert, tried to do the same, but with less success. The part he played in building up the reputation of the monarchy is recognized today. But the British of his own time never quite accepted him, because he was a foreigner.

Victoria only took the title of Empress—Empress of India—when her reign was halfway over, in 1876. But its splendor reflects the way in which Britain's power and wealth grew throughout the Victorian age.

Social reforms

Victorian Britain is also remembered, though, for its dreadful slums. These were not new to the great cities, but it was in the Victorian period that the press and public leaders first began to notice them. Reformers like Lord Shaftesbury campaigned for the removal of social evils and at the same time the poor themselves were beginning to work for improvements. Education was seen as an important way of achieving social reforms, and many schools were built. Although "Victorian values" are now criticized for their strictness, many changes were taking place behind the scenes.

Victoria herself is often thought of now as a grim old lady. But she was interested in the arts, in helping to spread education, and, according to her own letters, in reducing the power of the aristocracy. (Unlike many other rulers of her period, she was not aristocratic in outlook, and believed that most members of the upper classes were lazy, thoughtless, and immoral.) She loved animals, enjoyed a joke and, given the social climate of her time, she could be surprisingly broad-minded about people or behavior that her subjects would have disapproved of.

Her reputation for grimness mainly comes from her reaction to Prince Albert's death in 1861. She loved him deeply, and she was so grief stricken that she hid herself away for several years. From then on, the image grew of the Widow of Windsor, swathed in black and completely cheerless.

Throughout most of her long reign she continued to be popular. When she died in 1901, the whole nation went into mourning. People felt that both the old queen and the old century were now dead, and Britain and its empire would never be the same again. In fact the empire had yet to reach its greatest extent, and the Edwardian period would be remembered as a golden age. But more changes were on the way.

◄ In the early hours of the morning of June 20, 1837, Victoria—then aged 18—was awakened to be told that her uncle, William IV, was dead and that she was now queen. As this picture shows, the scene became a favorite with Victorian artists. Until she was 11, Victoria did not realize she would one day rule Britain. Upon finding out, she is reported to have said, "I will be good."

▲ During Victoria's reign, British soldiers often took part in wars abroad. Among these was the Crimean War against Russia (1854-6). It was during this war that the Charge of the Light Brigade took place. The troops knew the charge would be suicide, but they were ordered to advance regardless. Out of 673 men, 113 were killed and 134 wounded.

◀ An historic photograph of four British monarchs, showing Victoria with the late Edward VII, George V, and Edward VIII.

▲ Poverty in the city slums of Victorian Britain. There was a huge gulf between the rich and the poor. At the poorest level of society children like these not only had no permanent shelter or source of food, but they might well have no one at all to care for them. Barefoot and sleeping on the ground in any corner they could find, they spent their days trying to obtain food from wherever they could.

▼ The British Empire reached its greatest extent shortly after Victoria's reign. By this point, just after World War I, Canada, New Zealand, Australia and South Africa had dominion — or equal, rather than colonial status.

The British Empire

▲ Britain's influence in the world was envied by other power-seeking countries, as shown in this 1880s French cartoon. It depicts British influence over Egypt.

How Great Britain has changed

Benefiting from the boom

When Queen Victoria died, Britain was still one of the world's great powers. Little more than half a century later, its empire had vanished and its international prestige had been greatly reduced. But, by then, life was better than it had ever been for the vast majority of the British people.

Britain's welfare state—planned during World War II and introduced after it—brought together and improved the reforms of earlier periods. These reforms included early versions of unemployment pay and health insurance, along with pensions for the elderly. Both left and right wing governments remembered the appalling unemployment of the 1930s, and were determined not to let this happen again.

In some areas British industry had benefited from wartime inventions, and living standards were improving. Household appliances like washing machines and television sets had, by the 1960s, come within the reach of average families. Young people also benefited from the economic boom.

Record unemployment

At the start of the 1970s, most people expected their prosperity to continue. But at the same time there was accelerating inflation. The situation was soon made much worse by the oil crisis of 1973, when the oil-producing nations exerted pressure to increase the price of oil. Oil prices soared, and other prices did the same. Industrial demand slackened. In Britain, as elsewhere, there was unemployment on the scale remembered and feared from the 1930s. In Britain, the unemployment figure for January, 1986, stood at 3,407,729: the highest ever recorded. In the same month, government research suggested that the British were, on the average, better off than they used to be even in the early 1970s. Income levels were up; so was life expectancy. Working hours were down.

But the pattern of Britain's industry had changed (see pages 28–29), and the ever-growing army of unemployed people were victims of these changes.

▲ The "Swinging Sixties" in London. Britain's growing affluence had by the 1960s dramatically altered the social position of its young people. Instead of following their parents' styles, they now created their own and set their stamp on the world by establishing fashions and styles which were followed internationally. The best known shopping center of the period, Carnaby Street (shown here), is still popular with tourists.

◄ British miners drilling holes for explosives in a coal face. Britain's big coal deposits launched the Industrial Revolution. Coal remained Britain's main fuel until 20 years ago, when cheap oil became a major alternative. Now coal production has fallen to half the 1950 level, and an enormous number of miners have lost their jobs.

▼ Many traditional British industries, such as mining and steel making, are in decline. But others are growing and, of these, the new electronics industry is one of the most successful. In the Scottish factory shown here, circuit boards are being tested.

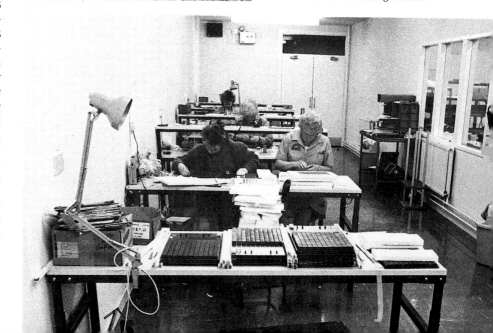

Will I find a job today? Britain, like many industrial countries, is suffering from large-scale unemployment, and many young people are facing a grim future in which they may never work.

▼ London during bombing raids in World War II. St. Paul's Cathedral survived, and so did Britain. Afterwards people were determined to make a world that was better to live in than the pre-war one.

▲ All lined up and ready to go: cars on the dockside awaiting export. But this dock is not in Britain, one of the traditional homes of the auto industry. It is in Japan—now one of the world's leading manufacturers of motor vehicles. After reaching a peak in 1972, British car manufacturing has now dwindled to less than half of its former output, while car imports have shot up. As a result, over 180,000 jobs have been lost in the industry.

The arts past and present

A literary nation

Britain is a literary nation. There have been important British composers, painters, and architects, but it is in literature that the British arts have reached their highest point. And, within literature, one man alone has ensured Britain's reputation as the greatest producer of drama in the world. William Shakespeare lived almost 400 years ago, but the action and excitement of his plays still make a huge impact on audiences everywhere.

The strength of Britain's literary tradition continues today, with more plays being written than can ever be staged. One important outlet for British playwrights is television. Television plays by such writers as Dennis Potter and Alan Bennett are praised all over the world. Televised versions of Shakespeare, and of novels by Trollope and others, have also been much acclaimed. International fame has also greeted the products of Britain's newly revived film industry, films like *Chariots of Fire* and *Gandhi*.

Passionate admirers

After drama, the novel is the greatest British contribution to the arts. The works of the great 19th century novelists like Charles Dickens, Jane Austen, and Thomas Hardy can be read again and again with increasing enjoyment.

The members of another and much older literary tradition are almost as famous. From Chaucer onward, British poets have inspired deep love and devotion. Donne, Pope, Keats, Shelley, Rupert Brooke, and Stevie Smith all have their passionate admirers. And this passion is shared by lovers of two other forms of art: that practiced by British painters, from Constable to David Hockney, and by British composers, from Purcell to Benjamin Britten and Michael Tippett.

▲ William Shakespeare (1564–1616). This is the nearest we have to an authentic portrait of the playwright. Little is known about his life.

▼ These street performers in London are following a long standing British tradition: in early days, actors also performed out-of-doors, in inn courtyards. Modern street theater, which turns its back on costly productions and brings drama to casual passersby, plays a recognized part in the modern British art scene.

◀ Robert Burns (1759–1796): farm laborer, customs man, and Scotland's national poet. Although renowned even in his own lifetime, he was usually very poor. His fame now extends far beyond Scotland.

▲ Joseph Mallord William Turner (1775–1851) used semi-abstract painting techniques to express the forces of nature. As shown in this picture of the *Fighting Téméraire,* he was fascinated by the power and effects of light.

▼ A Welsh harpist leads a group of country dancers and singers. Wales has a strong and quite distinct artistic tradition, centering mainly on music and the Welsh language. The national *Eistedfodd* is a festival of Welsh music and poetry.

▲ The great Victorian novelist Charles Dickens (1812–1870) created some of the most vividly-drawn characters in English fiction. The best known of his works is possibly *Oliver Twist,* but *Great Expectations, The Pickwick Papers,* and *A Christmas Carol*—with its anti-hero, Scrooge—are close runners up. He fearlessly attacked the attitudes held by the people in power at the time towards the poor, the unfortunate, and the vulnerable in society. He even criticized the treatment of criminals.

Heroes of fact and fiction

defended Britain against Saxon invaders in about AD 516—to Britain's leader in World War II, Winston Churchill. Other great warrior heroes who really lived include Robert the Bruce of Scotland, General Wolfe, and Lord Nelson.

The great tradition

At the center of much British art is the Great British Hero: real-life, legendary, or completely fictional. The British have a rich tradition of heroes, and the heroic qualities they admire include courage, energy, and a willingness to risk all to protect the underdog—the poor, the threatened, or the hopelessly outnumbered. The heroic line stretches from King Arthur—who may have

Romantic failures

Oddly enough, failure does not stop someone from being seen as a hero. An even older hero—or, rather, heroine—than King Arthur is the Celtic queen Boudicca, who tried to throw the Romans out of Britain in AD 61. She lost, but her name is still famous almost 2,000 years later. Again, Bonnie Prince Charlie failed in his attempt to win the British crown in 1745. But he is still thought of as a glamorous, romantic figure.

Another sort of British hero is admired for his daring, his style, and his quick wit. Robin Hood, the outlaw who robbed the rich to give to the poor, is one sort of heroic thief; so is the highwayman Dick Turpin.

▼ Some of Britain's heroes, like King Arthur, are shadowy figures, half real and half legendary. But many others, like the British naval commander Lord Nelson, clearly belong to the real world. Trafalgar Square in London commemorates his last victory and his death in 1805.

◄ When the man who might have been the real King Arthur died, people began to tell a great many stories about him. Some were true, some were not, and some were true but were really about other people. In this way, Arthur is remembered both as a (possibly) real person and as a legendary one. A lot of the best known tales about the king and his warriors come from the Middle Ages and, as shown here, are about beautiful maidens, witch queens, and knights in shining armor.

Sherlock Holmes, unlike King Arthur, was a fictional figure from the start. He was created in the late Victorian period by Sir Arthur Conan Doyle, and quickly became the most famous detective in all literature. His genius for clue spotting came from meticulous observation and a remarkable memory. He is shown here vanquishing the Hound of the Baskervilles. In the end, Conan Doyle got tired of Holmes and tried to kill him off. But this horrified Holmes fans so much that the author had to bring his creation back to life. Even today, the great detective is so much admired that some people act as if Holmes really existed. His rather plodding companion, Dr. Watson, is also famous.

▲ "Winnie": Winston Churchill, the most recent of Britain's great hero figures, and Prime Minister during World War II. His bulldog image and his determination symbolized the country's will to survive.

▼ The British hero tradition is strong enough to absorb characters from other cultures and make them its own. Mr. Punch—another anti-hero we love to hate—started life as Punchinello a figure from the 16th century Italian stage. He always dressed in white and wore a pointed hat.

I'D MOVE, ONLY I'M ONE OF THE GOAL-POSTS!

A modern version of the Great British anti-hero. The deplorable attitudes of cartoon figure Andy Capp are a long way from the high ideals of King Arthur or Holmes. Andy is lazy, deceitful, work-shy, selfish and, as here, he bullies his wife Flo. (She often bullies him back.) In fact, he belongs to still another British hero tradition: the sly trickster. Andy also represents a stereotype of someone from northern Britain.

Inventors and discoverers

The inquisitive urge

It is no surprise that the British, who invented the basic technology that launched the Industrial Revolution, should be famous for inventions in general. They are also famous as discoverers and explorers, working in territory that ranges from unmapped oceans to still mysterious areas of the human body and its workings.

The inquisitive, exploring urge of the British goes back a long way. In the 1500s, Francis Drake sailed around the world. In the 17th century, Henry Hudson gave his name to Hudson Bay in Canada, and William Harvey discovered how blood circulates in the human body. Later in the same century, Isaac Newton discovered the law of gravity.

Travelers' inventions

Many of the British inventions have been in the field of transportation, from the chronometer to the railways, and much more recently, the hovercraft. The chronometer was invented by John Harrison. It is the super-accurate clock essential to sailors wanting to calculate their course by the principles of navigation. The first practical steamship was the Scottish *Charlotte Dundas* of 1801. The first heavier-than-air machine to actually fly was a model glider built in 1804 by George Cayley. (In 1853, his coachman was the first to fly in a heavier-than-air machine.) In 1894, engineer Charles Parsons revolutionized sea travel and steamships by inventing the steam turbine engine. And, through early developments in city transportation, London was by then becoming the world's first giant metropolis.

▲ Isaac Newton (1642–1727) using prism to find out about the properties of light. Newton made many important contributions to scientific knowledge, among them the law of gravity.

▲ Moving photographs were first shown in the late 19th century, but only in the cinema. It was a Scottish engineer, John Logie Baird, who brought them into people's living rooms. On January 26, 1926, television pictures, transmitted through his mechanical television process, were first demonstrated to scientists. But his system was later scrapped.

▶ Before the development of antibiotics, infections were dreaded killers. But, in 1928, Sir Alexander Fleming noticed a mold growing in a dish containing a disease-causing bacteria. Fleming observed that the mold had destroyed the bacteria. Fleming's discovery led to the development of the first practical antibiotic, penicillin. Others followed, and many killer diseases can now be cured.

Michael Faraday (1791–1867) made
ances in chemistry, physics and electric-
The genesis of electrical engineering goes
ck to his discovery of electro-magnetic
uction in 1831.

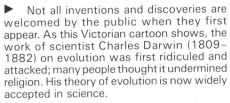 Not all inventions and discoveries are
welcomed by the public when they first
appear. As this Victorian cartoon shows, the
work of scientist Charles Darwin (1809–
1882) on evolution was first ridiculed and
attacked; many people thought it undermined
religion. His theory of evolution is now widely
accepted in science.

▼ The hovercraft is a modern British development in both sea and land travel. Invented
by Christopher Cockerell, it moves on a cush-
ion of air and can travel over water or land.

What Britain has to sell

Oil, computers, and the "invisibles"

Britain is a small island with a large urban population. To buy the food and raw materials that it does not produce it must sell its own products abroad, and these mainly take the form of manufactured goods.

In the 19th century, when this trading arrangement evolved, Britain was called the "workshop of the world." Although later rivaled (and passed) by other countries, it has continued to rely heavily on sales of manufactured goods right up to the present decade. Now, however, its trading pattern has undergone a radical change, and it imports more manufactured goods than it exports. But it also spends less money on food imports than it used to, and less on raw materials. Its fuel imports have gone up but, at the same time, the presence of its own North Sea oil allows it to sell more fuel than it buys.

Although there has been a steep drop in demand for British industry's traditional products (such as steel and textiles, engineering products, cars, ships, and aircraft), some areas of work have been growing. One is the computer industry. Others are insurance and banking. Services like banking are part of what is called "invisible trade" and are an important source of income for Britain. Tourism is another major invisible: the millions of people who visit the country each year are buying the experience of being in Britain, using their own countries' money to do so.

▲ Britain is a leading exporter of style for people of all ages. Laura Ashley clothes, with their reminders of country gardens, sell all over the world. This Laura Ashley shop is in New York.

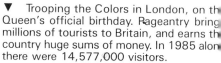
▼ Trooping the Colors in London, on the Queen's official birthday. Pageantry brings millions of tourists to Britain, and earns the country huge sums of money. In 1985 alone there were 14,577,000 visitors.

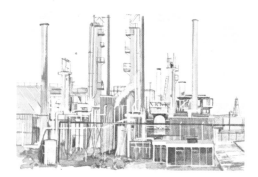

▲ The chemical industry is a major pillar of the British economy. It has suffered much less from the decline in manufacturing than have the traditional British industries such as textile making.

▲ Dark-suited "city gents" mob the floor at London's Stock Exchange. Britain is one of the world's leading financial markets. Handling money transactions brings Britain a lot of foreign business.

▼ All over the world, British pottery is famous for its superb standards of craftsmanship. It is still made in many traditional styles. Here, skilled workers are painting intricate designs by hand.

▲ Since the discovery of oil in the North Sea, Britain has become an important oil producing country. But people are worried about what will happen when the oil runs out.

London: the capital city

The founding of London

Britain's capital city, London, was established in the 1st century AD by the Romans. The new town, which Britain's conquerors called Londinium, grew up on the site of the present City of London. This was the nearest convenient point to the sea, where a bridge—the first London Bridge—could be built across the River Thames.

London grew from a small bridgehead settlement into a big city. The river and its bridge brought transportation and trade; prestige came when King Edward the Confessor built a palace and an abbey along the river at the neighboring settlement of Westminster. Once these two settlements had been joined together by buildings, London started growing outward, taking in many outlying villages on the way. Together with its suburbs, 20th century London measures 36 miles across, and is the seventeenth largest city in the world. It now has a population of nearly seven million.

London's violent history

Like many other capital cities, London has had a violent history. It has been attacked or burned several times, the last time during the bombing raids of World War II. The most famous London blaze was the Great Fire of 1666, which started in a corner of the city and destroyed nearly all of it. Sir Christopher Wren built the present St. Paul's Cathedral to replace the one that was burned.

Things to see in London

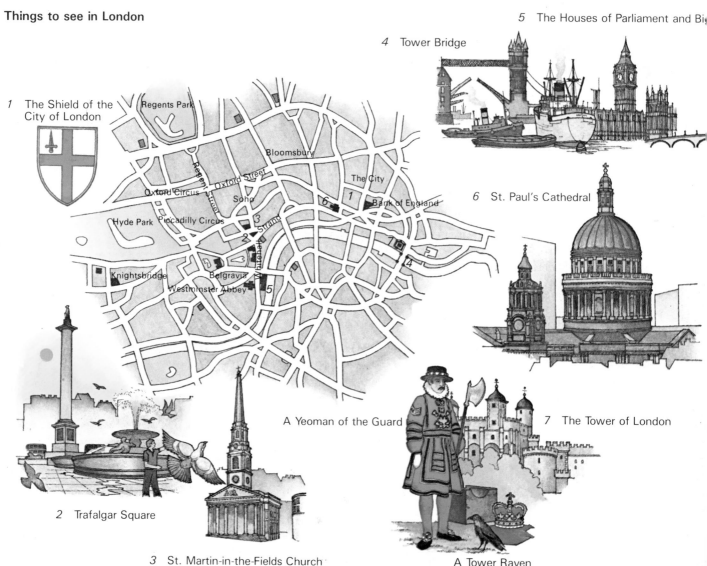

1 The Shield of the City of London

2 Trafalgar Square

3 St. Martin-in-the-Fields Church

4 Tower Bridge

5 The Houses of Parliament and Big

6 St. Paul's Cathedral

7 The Tower of London

A Yeoman of the Guard

A Tower Raven

The heart of London today: the City, and the Strand that was its first link with Westminster; the fashionable districts of Knightsbridge and Belgravia; Soho, famous for its restaurants; Oxford Street, always packed with shoppers; the intellectual quarter of Bloomsbury, home of the British Museum; and five of London's parks. Most theaters are situated between Oxford Street and the Strand.

▲ View of the City of London from the South Bank of the River Thames. The dome of St. Paul's Cathedral, masterpiece of the architect Sir Christopher Wren, is dwarfed by modern office buildings.

▼ Leicester Square, in the heart of London's entertainment and nightlife districts. Part of the square is barred to traffic, so people can stroll about freely.

▲ The Serpentine Lake in Hyde Park is close to the very center of London, but it can make Londoners feel as if they are in the country. London has many parks.

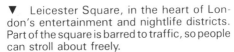

▲ Leather, studs, and startling hairstyles are the trademark of London's famous punks. Once seen as threatening, punk styles now attract the attention of tourists and their cameras.

31

Cloudy skies and green, green gardens

Can we walk on it?

One of the first things summer visitors to Britain notice is the greenness of the landscape. And the sights they look for include the lush, scented gardens that surround many British homes. The British lawn, carefully mown into a pattern of pale and dark green stripes, is especially famous. "Can we walk on it?" is the question visitors often ask, and are delighted that they can. Visitors may be surprised to find grapes ripening under cloudy skies and palm trees in a country which is on the same latitude as Newfoundland.

Moist, mild, and moderate

The reason for these surprises and for the general fame of Britain's gardens lies in another of Britain's famous features: its weather. Typical British weather is moist and mild. (The warm Gulf Stream current flowing past Britain's west coast helps to keep winter temperatures up.)

This moderate climate allows Britain's gardeners to grow plants that come from all over the world, from the Himalayas to the Mediterranean. But the British climate is also very changeable. So gardeners and farmers always have to be ready to protect their more delicate plants from sudden frosts.

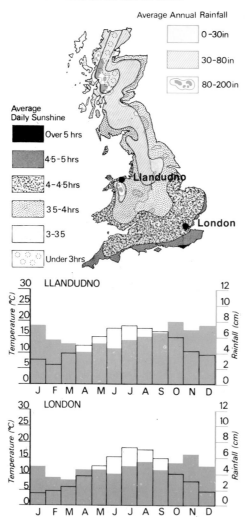

The climate of Great Britain

Average Annual Rainfall

☐ 0-30in
▨ 30-80in
⬭ 80-200in

Average Daily Sunshine

■ Over 5 hrs
▦ 4·5-5 hrs
▥ 4-4·5hrs
▨ 3·5-4hrs
☐ 3-3·5
⠂ Under 3hrs

LLANDUDNO

LONDON

▲ Britain's weather becomes sunnier and drier the farther one goes south and east, as shown by the rainfall columns in the two charts.

▲ Prevailing winds over Britain come from the southwest, across the Atlantic, and bring plenty of moisture with them. It usually falls as rain; snow is fairly unusual.

▼ Florida? Actually, this is a vacation resort in England. In the south, summer temperatures start at around 65°F, and can go higher. The changeability of the climate, turning to rain with little warning, can be a problem for vacationers.

▲ The Albert Memorial, commemorating Queen Victoria's husband, is in one of the best loved of London's parks, Kensington Gardens. There are velvety green lawns and sheets of daffodils in March. To do well daffodils need lots of moisture in spring.

◄ The snow-covered north face of Ben Nevis in the northwest of Scotland. It is Britain's highest mountain and stands at 4,406 feet above sea level. There can be snow on it for a great part of the year.

▼ Plants from the southern hemisphere grow with palm trees in Inverewe Gardens, even farther north than Ben Nevis. But the sea and the warm Gulf Stream current flowing up from the Caribbean keep the climate mild.

Homes and households

Pride in ownership

Home ownership is a British ideal, and the ideal home is usually a house, with its own front door and a garden for children to play in. The number of British homes that are actually owned, rather than rented, by their tenants has risen sharply since World War II and now stands at almost two-thirds of the total. Less than a third are rented from local councils, and this number is steadily falling as tenants buy the council homes that they live in.

Two up, two down

The typical style for older housing in England and Wales is the two-up-two-down terrace: a street of identical houses, each with two rooms on each of its two floors. Streets of terraced houses are found all over the country, built of materials that differ according to the area and age of the street. Many have been enlarged, with a loft extension in the attic. In Scotland the tradition is for apartments, or flats, in large buildings. Another common building style is the semi-detached, two-family home in the suburbs.

A government survey in 1983 showed that over half of British households are made up of married couples and their children. Nearly a quarter of the households are made up of single people living on their own.

The British are informal and friendly, as long as their privacy is respected. Their homes are above all places to escape from the world outside.

▲ Terraced homes like these, with a garden, are typical of the inner areas of many British cities. They are now often divided into several self-contained apartments.

◄ Three years old today: a family meets to celebrate the birthday of a young member. Not every family has a garden, but those who do take every opportunity to be out in them — weather permitting.

34

Christmas dinner with roast turkey and a ch plum pudding is a traditional British meal, nd for many families it is one of the main ighlights of the year. Festivals are an impor-ant time for family gatherings.

▲ Shopping—for the day or the week? Supermarkets have revolutionized British shopping habits because of the types of processed and packaged foods they offer. Their prices are often lower than those in smaller shops.

▼ Doing things around the house and garden is a typically British way of spending leisure time. Here, the family car gets its turn.

▼ How the average British household spent its money in 1984. Spending on housing and transportation (as a proportion of total household spending) has gone up since the 1960s.

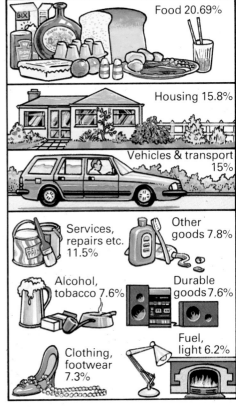

Food 20.69%

Housing 15.8%

Vehicles & transport 15%

Services, repairs etc. 11.5%

Other goods 7.8%

Alcohol, tobacco 7.6%

Durable goods 7.6%

Clothing, footwear 7.3%

Fuel, light 6.2%

Eating the British way

Changing habits

Until recently, British food had an undeserved reputation for dullness. During the war years, many foods were in short supply, and plain food became the norm. However, Elizabethan cooking was famous, and so was that of the Edwardian era at the beginning of our century. But many servants were needed to cook and serve an Edwardian dinner of 12 courses. As fewer people became prepared to be servants, meals began to be simpler.

The basic British cooking tradition relies heavily on foods that are boiled, baked, or fried: cakes, puddings, chips, and "bangers-and-mash" (sausages and mashed potato) are some of them. But this tradition is also changing. The British are becoming more health conscious, and more and more people are trying to cut down on the amount of heavy, fatty food they eat. Also many married women work outside the home as well as look after their families. They often find it easier to buy food that is already prepared and packaged, rather than make traditional dishes.

▶ Like much old-style food, the traditional cheeses of Britain are on the solid side. Cheddar and Stilton are the best known. Others which are easily available are Leicester, Double Gloucester, Derby and Wensleydale. Caerphilly is a mild white hard cheese which originated in Wales. Cheese with pickles and bread makes the modern pub meal known as a "plowman's lunch."

Typical meals for a day

The workday breakfast usually consists of cereals, toast, and tea or coffee.

Lunch is often a quick meal, such as sausages and baked beans with tea or coffee.

Evening dinner is the main meal, eaten as early as 6 pm, or much later. A favorite is traditional steak and kidney pie; it can be bought ready-made and frozen.

▼ The cultures meet in this take-out restaurant: customers either have a Turkish-style kebab, or follow the British tradition and opt for fish and chips. Ethnic restaurants now flourish, catering to Britain's increasingly varied tastes in food.

▲ Roast beef, Yorkshire pudding, roast potatoes, and Brussels sprouts make up the classic main dish of the traditional Sunday lunch. The roast beef of old England is among the most famous of Britain's dishes; its Yorkshire accompaniment is almost as celebrated.

▲ Haggis is a Scottish speciality. It is made of offal, suet, onions, oatmeal and seasoning, all stuffed into a sheep's stomach, like a giant sausage. It is traditionally served on Burns' Night, when the Scots celebrate their national poet, Robert Burns.

36

XED VEGETABLE SOUP

b mixed vegetables (potato, onion, turnip,
rrot)
oz fat
pints hot stock
asoning
oz oatmeal or rolled oats
pint milk
rsley

op the vegetables finely. Melt the fat and
n them in it. Add the stock and seasoning.
ng to a boil, then simmer until the vegeta-
s are tender. Then stir in the oatmeal or
led oats with milk and cook, stirring, for ten
nutes more. Add the chopped parsley
en serving.

SHEPHERD'S PIE

1 lb potatoes
2 teaspoons of milk
lump of butter or margarine
1 chopped onion
dripping or lard
½ lb cooked chopped meat
¼ pint hot stock
herbs and seasoning

Boil the potatoes; strain, then mash them,
using milk, butter and seasoning. Fry the
onion in dripping or lard; stir in the chopped
meat and fry it lightly; then add the stock, seasoning and herbs. Put the meat mixture in a
pie dish and cover it with mashed potato.
Make a pattern in the potato with a fork, add a
few pats of butter or margarine, and heat it in a
medium oven for half an hour.

BAKED APPLES AND CUSTARD

4 large cooking apples
1 tablespoon golden syrup
1 oz brown sugar
2 oz dried fruit

Wash the apples and cut out the cores using
an apple corer or small knife. Fill hole in each
apple with syrup, sugar and dried fruit. Place
in a greased dish with a little water and bake in
a medium oven until tender.

Custard

2 tablespoons custard powder
1 oz sugar, 1 pint cold milk, few drops
vanilla essence

Make the custard, following the instructions
on the package. Serve with baked apples.

▲ Britain is an island nation, and seafood
forms an important part of the British diet.
Shellfish are cheap and nutritious, so whelks,
cockles, mussels, and eels are among the traditional foods of London's East End. Whelk
stalls are now also a tourist attraction.

Education in Britain

Universal education

British parents are required by law to see that their children receive efficient full-time education between the ages of 5 and 16. For all parents who wish it, this education is free: that is, it is provided as a public service, and paid for through taxation.

This free system of education—which, of course, is paid for by all rate- and tax-payers, whether they are parents or not—is usually called the state system, and dates back to the late 19th century. (Free elementary education for almost all children was introduced in 1891.) It exists alongside the separate, and much smaller, system of independent schools, for which most pupils' parents pay fees. The independent system includes such famous public schools as Eton and Harrow. In 1984 there were just under nine million pupils in state schools, and half a million in independent schools.

In state schools in England and Wales, pupils usually move from primary to secondary school when they are 11. (In Scotland—which has a separate system—they move up at 12.) Until the 1970s, most pupils took an exam called the 11-plus, which decided what sort of secondary school they went to. Only the brightest were allowed to go on to an academic education. Today, almost all pupils in the state system throughout Great Britain go to the same sort of secondary school: the comprehensive. This takes children of all abilities.

▲ A science lesson taking place in a Scottish secondary school. The Scottish education system is slightly different from that of England and Wales.

◀ Plenty of room to play in this modern urban primary school. Primary education is a child's first experience of formal schooling; teaching methods integrate both play and study.

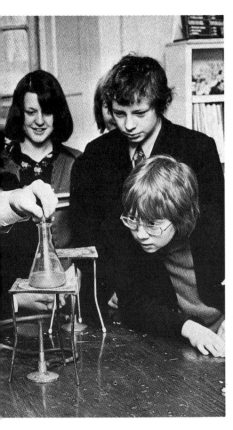

"No talking" used to be the rule. But in schools today, like this secondary one, discussion is encouraged and pupils can consult the teacher and each other.

Students at Cambridge University. In 1983, 292,000 young people went on after school to study full time at universities. In England alone, almost two million more went to other types of colleges.

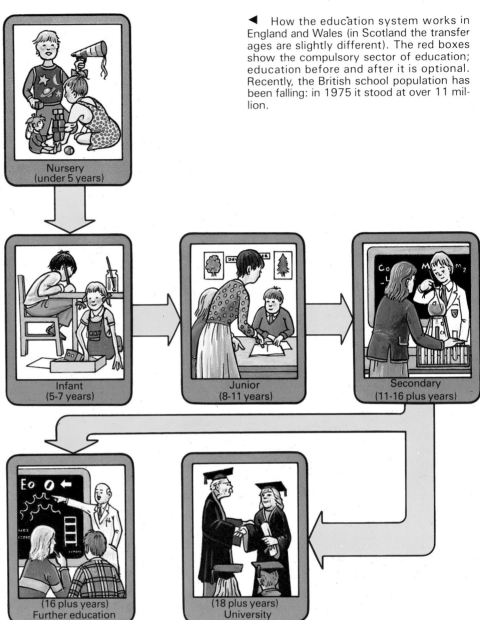

◀ How the education system works in England and Wales (in Scotland the transfer ages are slightly different). The red boxes show the compulsory sector of education; education before and after it is optional. Recently, the British school population has been falling: in 1975 it stood at over 11 million.

Nursery (under 5 years)

Infant (5-7 years)

Junior (8-11 years)

Secondary (11-16 plus years)

(16 plus years) Further education

(18 plus years) University

Time off: leisure and pleasure

Home-based pursuits

The average working week in Britain is now 37–38 hours. Although several hours' traveling time should be added to this total, it still allows the British a good amount of leisure time. How do they like to spend their time off?

Although a wide variety of leisure pursuits is available—from grand opera for London dwellers to walking in the countryside—a few favorites have topped the list for well over ten years. Most popular of all is watching television: in a government survey in 1983, at least 97 percent of the people asked, said they had watched television in the previous month. Other favorites are also home-based: gardening, listening to tapes or records, working on the house, and—for many women—

needlework and knitting. Going down to the pub is another popular leisure activity (especially for men). But going out for a meal is seen as a luxury.

The great outdoors

In Britain, the countryside is almost always within reach, and 61 percent of households have a car. But people are less anxious to go out in it than they used to be.

Thanks to television, many outdoor sports are also enjoyed indoors, from the very popular soccer to sheepdog trials. But the new interest in health has meant that the British do go outdoors for pursuits like walking and jogging.

▲ Cricket is sometimes called the English national game; it is certainly one of Britain's greatest and most popular exports to the rest of the world. In Britain itself, it is known to have been played in some form from about the middle of the 16th century. Some games can take up to five days, although one-day matches are also played.

Shopping for necessities can be a chore, [bu]t shopping for leisure equipment is a favor[ite] pastime for the whole family. Here, even [th]e baby seems intrigued by the electronic [ga]mes.

▲ Contestants for the snooker world championships line up for the television cameras. After walking, snooker is the next most popular sport among British men.

▼ A British pub or public house, for centuries a center for relaxation and entertainment. The attractions include good beer and cheerful companionship.

Over a quarter of British vacationers go [ab]road for their vacations. Among those who [st]ay, active vacations such as camping, boat[in]g, and walking are great favorites.

A rugby football match between [W]ales—in the red shirts—and Japan. Rugby [is] another of Britain's important sports.

Reference

FACTS AND FIGURES

The land and people
Full title: United Kingdom of Great Britain and Northern Ireland.

Position: Between 50°N and 60°N and 2°E and 8°W. Largest island of Europe, lying north-west of the continent of Europe. Closest neighbors are France, Belgium, and the Netherlands.

Constituent parts: Great Britain comprises England, Scotland, and Wales. The United Kingdom also includes Northern Ireland. The Isle of Man and the Channel Islands are not strictly part of the UK, but are dependencies of the Crown.

Area: England 50,335 sq. miles (130,367 sq. km), Scotland 30,414 sq. miles (78,772 sq. km), and Wales 8,011 sq. miles (20,764 sq. km).

Population: (1981) England 46,362,836; Scotland 5,130,735; Wales 2,791,851.

Capital: London, pop. 6,776,000 (1981).

Language: English, but in Wales 503,559 (1981) spoke Welsh. In Scotland at the same date 79,307 spoke Gaelic.

Religions: Church of England (Protestant Episcopal), approx. 1,700,000 members (1982). Church of Scotland, approx. 900,000 members (1983). Methodist Church, 487,000 members (1984). Roman Catholic Church, approx. 5,000,000 (1984). Jewish, approx. 354,000 (1984).

Political system: Constitutional monarchy. Continuous monarchy from 802, except for Commonwealth 1649-60. Supreme legislative authority is the Queen in Parliament (the Queen and the two Houses of Parliament). Constitution unwritten.

Head of State: Her Majesty Queen Elizabeth II, Head of the Commonwealth and Defender of the Faith.

Armed Forces: (1984) 325,100; Army 161,000; Navy 71,000; Air Force 93,000. The USA has air and naval bases in Britain.

International organizations: Member of the United Nations, the Commonwealth, the European Economic Community (EEC), the North Atlantic Treaty Organization (NATO), and the Organization for Economic Cooperation and Development (OECD).

The unwritten constitution: The British system of government has evolved through many hundreds of years. It has been changed constantly to meet changing requirements. The sovereign once had complete power, but is now said to "reign but not rule." The UK is governed by her Majesty's Government *in the name of the Queen.*

The two Houses
The British Parliament consists of two parts: the House of Lords and the elected House of Commons. Their job is the same: to pass laws, to make finance available, and to put important issues before the electorate. But the Commons, which is elected by almost all citizens over 18 years, is the real seat of parliamentary power.

The Government
The political party which has the most Members of the House of Commons elected in a general election forms the government. Its leader becomes the Prime Minister and chooses the members of the government. The most important ministers form the Cabinet, which makes government policy. But the Cabinet must have the support of its party both in Parliament and the country.

History

Kings and Queens of England
Saxons and Danes
802–39	Egbert
839–58	Ethelwulf
858–60	Ethelbald
860–6	Ethelbert
866–71	Ethelred
871–99	Alfred the Great
899–924	Edward the Elder
924–40	Aethelstan
940–6	Edmund
946–55	Edred
955–9	Edwy
959–75	Edgar
975–8	Edward the Martyr
978–1016	Ethelred the Unready
1016	Edmund Ironside
1016–35	Canute the Dane
1035–40	Harold I
1040–2	Harthacnut
1042–66	Edward the Confessor
1066	Harold II

House of Normandy
1066–87	William I (the Conqueror)
1087–1100	William II
1100–35	Henry I
1135–54	Stephen

House of Plantagenet
1154–89	Henry II
1189–99	Richard I (Lionheart)
1199–1216	John
1216–72	Henry III
1272–1307	Edward I
1307–27	Edward II
1327–77	Edward III
1377–99	Richard II

House of Lancaster
1399–1413	Henry IV
1413–22	Henry V
1422–61	Henry VI

House of York
1461–83	Edward IV
1483	Edward V
1483–5	Richard III

House of Tudor
1485–1509	Henry VII
1509–47	Henry VIII
1547–53	Edward VI
1553–8	Mary Tudor (Mary I)
1558–1603	Elizabeth I

House of Stuart
1603–25	James I
1625–49	Charles I
[1649–60]	**Commonwealth** (No king
1660–85	Charles II
1685–8	James II
1689–94	William III and Mary II
1694–1702	William III
1702–14	Anne

House of Hanover
1714–27	George I
1727–60	George II
1760–1820	George III
1820–30	George IV
1830–7	William IV
1837–1901	Victoria

House of Saxe-Coburg
1901–10	Edward VII

House of Windsor
1910–36	George V
1936	Edward VIII
1936–52	George VI
1952–	Elizabeth II

Scottish Kings and Queens 1057–160
1057–93	Malcolm III (Canmore)
1093	Donald Ban
1094	Duncan II
1094–7	Donald Ban (restored)
1097–1107	Edgar
1107–24	Alexander I
1124–53	David I
1153–65	Malcolm V (The Maiden)
1165–1214	William I
1214–49	Alexander II
1249–86	Alexander III
1286–90	Margaret, Maid of Norwa
1292–6	John Baliol
1306–29	Robert I (Bruce)
1329–71	David II
1371–90	Robert II ("the Steward")
1390–1406	Robert III
1406–37	James I
1437–60	James II
1460–88	James III
1488–1513	James IV
1513–42	James V
1542–87	Mary
1587–1625	James VI (became king England 1603)

ENGLAND, SCOTLAND & WALES : Physical

Cities and Towns
International Boundaries
Internal Boundaries
Mountain Peaks ▲ 1887 metres

feet	metres
3000	914
1000	305
500	152
0	0

Scale 1:3,700,000

0 20 40 60 miles
0 40 80 kilometres

Projection : Conical with 2 standard parallels

Un same scale as main map

West from Greenwich 0 East from Greenwich